1954

BRITAIN IN PICTURES
THE BRITISH PEOPLE IN PICTURES

BRITISH HILLS AND MOUNTAINS

GENERAL EDITOR
W. J. TURNER

The Editor is most grateful to all those who have
so kindly helped in the selection of illustrations
especially to officials of the various public
Museums Libraries and Galleries and
to all others who have generously
allowed pictures and MSS
to be reproduced

BRITISH
HILLS AND MOUNTAINS

PETER BICKNELL

WITH
8 PLATES IN COLOUR
AND
23 ILLUSTRATIONS IN
BLACK & WHITE

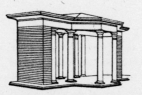

COLLINS · 14 ST. JAMES'S PLACE · LONDON
MCMXLVII

PRODUCED BY
ADPRINT LIMITED LONDON

PRINTED IN GREAT BRITAIN BY
CLARKE & SHERWELL LTD NORTHAMPTON
ON MELLOTEX BOOK PAPER MADE BY
TULLIS RUSSELL & CO LTD MARKINCH SCOTLAND

LIST OF ILLUSTRATIONS

PLATES IN COLOUR

BLACK AND WHITE ILLUSTRATIONS

ABER LLAN FROM PLAS GWYNANT
Pen drawing by Joshua Cristall, 1767-1847

INTRODUCTION

EVERY summer before the war I used to visit the Alps. I would
always return home with a vague feeling of disquiet. After the magnificence of the mountains would the little hills of this island have
lost their charm? Would the first distant view from Hartside of the Lakeland fells be anything but anti-climax after the glory of the Oberland seen
from the terrace at Berne? How could the gentle grass slopes of the downs
have anything to give after the snow and ice of Mont Blanc? How could
even the grandeur of the Cuillin seem anything but trivial after the cliffs
of the Matterhorn? Yearly I took the first opportunity of re-visiting the
hills. Yearly the same miracle was wrought. The hills were more beautiful
than ever. Their place in my affections was only deepened by the experience
of bigger mountains.

This affection for the hills is a very personal matter of memory and
association, and inevitably a personal note will appear in this book. But

it is an affection which I share with many thousands of my countrymen, each one of whom sees and enjoys the hills in his own particular way. Most Englishmen live far from anything more like a mountain than Primrose Hill. Scotland and Wales however are hill countries and there are few dwellings from which the Scot or the Welshman cannot lift up his eyes unto the hills. The South Wales mining villages are in once lovely mountain valleys. In the streets of Edinburgh the craggy form of Arthur's Seat or the outline of the Pentland Hills is ever present. But whether hills are in the blood or not there is a general love of the high places from Ben Nevis to Box Hill.

Of the many qualities that give our hills their own endearing beauty the greatest is variety—variety of form, colour and atmosphere. The fascinating history of the formation of the hills explains their infinite variety of shape and texture. Not only has every group its own character, as different as the Cairngorms from the Cotswolds, but in each separate group it is the juxtaposition of hills of different formation which increases the beauty of the landscape as a whole. The jagged peaks of the Black Cuillin are set in sharp relief against the rounded forms of the Red Cuillin. Leith Hill in the Weald looks out to the enclosing downs, completely different in formation and resulting flora. The smooth weathered shapes of Skiddaw and Saddleback are a foil to the rock architecture of Scafell and Gable. An outcrop of limestone produces a patch of brighter green ; a pocket of sand, a patch of heather, pines and furze. Little hills like the Malverns and the Wrekin rise in such striking contrast with the comparatively flat country in which they are set that they assume the character of real mountains. The hills are clothed with vegetation varying with climate and soil which displays in its changing colours the procession of the seasons. The moisture-laden atmosphere of this western isle lends distance to the mountain view and invests it with those soft transparent colours which fired the imagination of our great landscape painters. The sea plays a part in the view from almost every British hill. The distant silver shimmer on Bristol Channel, Cardigan Bay or Solway is familiar to all who know the hills. And where the sea has actually invaded the mountains the play of light on their flanks is enlivened by the reflection off the surface of the water. Most of our hills lie along the western seaboard where light and colour change with dazzling rapidity in the Atlantic air. Sunshine swiftly gives place to storm. Mists and clouds are as much a part of the mountain scene as the hills themselves, and sudden glimpses through the cloud transform and magnify the view.

Nowhere outside the British islands will one find such variety in so small a space.

8

SNOWDON

Water colour by John Varley, 1778 - 1842

FLANK OF SNOWDON

Oil painting by John Piper, 1945

THE HILLS

BRITAIN can be roughly divided into an upland and a lowland area by a line drawn from the mouth of the Tees to the mouth of the Exe. To the north and west of this line, where the underlying rocks are older than the coal measures, lie the main hill masses and moorlands ; to the south and east, where the underlying rocks are newer, hills are only minor incidents in an agricultural landscape. In the upland area there are three main groups of hills which are mountainous in character—the Highlands of Scotland, the mountains of Wales and the Lake District.

In Scotland the Highlands are divided from the Lowlands by a line, similar and more or less parallel to the Tees-Exe line, drawn from Stonehaven on the east coast to Helensburgh on the Clyde. It divides a land of mountains sparsely inhabited by hill-land clans of Celtic and Norse origin, from the richer more populous agricultural and industrial districts of the south—the land of the Anglo-Saxon invader. The Highlands and Islands are a mountain tableland, dissected and worn into a bewildering variety of shapes, but having throughout a certain uniformity of character.

In the west the climate is warm, windy and wet. As far north as Scourie, beyond the 58th degree of latitude, semi-tropical garden plants are grown. In the east it is colder and drier. Snow lies on the hills through the winter and spring. On Ben Nevis there is a small patch of snow which only disappears in exceptionally warm autumns; and one on the Cairngorms has not disappeared within living memory. Scotland would only have to be raised about 1,000 feet for there to be glacier conditions.

The Highlands are split in two by the Great Glen, the fault which so nearly makes the land to its north an island. South of it lie the highest hills and the greatest mountain masses in Britain. The southern fringe is so easily accessible from Glasgow and Perth, that every year thousands of workers are able to enjoy the beauties of Ben Lomond and the Trossachs, to climb on the gnarled rocks of the Cobbler and to wander in the Perthshire Hills.

Between the southern fringe and the Great Glen, the Grampians form a continuous belt of high land from the Argyll coast to the lower arable lands of Aberdeenshire. They are traversed by two historic lines of communication—to Fort William by the Moor of Rannoch and Glencoe and to Inverness by Killiecrankie and the Spey. At the western end of the Grampians are the hills of Lochaber. Ben Nevis, the highest, rises 4,406 feet in only four miles from the sea at Fort William. In shape it is the epitome of many British hills, rounded and easily accessible from the south, but cut off from the north by a tremendous series of precipices. In early spring it is a snow mountain, when in spite of its proximity to the sea, successive freezing and melting of the snow and ice on the crags and in the gullies develop conditions reminiscent of the Alps. South of Lochaber

9

KILCHURN CASTLE, LOCH AWE
Oil painting by Horatio McCulloch, 1839

lies Glencoe where the main road north passes down a defile flanked by terrific cliffs. Buchal Etive, the Shepherd, stands sentinel at its head, a lovely cone-shaped pile of rock rising out of that "desolate and extensive wild," the Moor of Rannoch.

East of the Inverness road lie the Cairngorms. Their character is something altogether different from that of any other British hills. They are on a far larger scale. The distances are vast. It is ten miles for the eagle to fly from Aviemore to Ben Macdhui. For twenty miles the main ridge is continuously over 3,000 feet above sea level but for one dip at the head of Glen Derry. Four of the tops are over 4,000 feet high. The outline of the hills is not dramatic, but they are cut into by deep rocky corries and glens, in which rise the head-waters of the most illustrious of salmon rivers, the Spey and the Dee. To the north-west lies Rothiemurchus forest, the only great surviving tract of the ancient pine forest which once covered most of the Highlands. To the south-east lies Deeside where conventional highland beauties are squandered with a royal prodigality. The Cairngorms are wild and magnificent at any time of the year. In winter they can be merciless, but they are at their kindest on a sunny April day when the snow is still on the hills and the fresh green birch is bursting from a haze of red buds and silver stems.

The watershed of the Northern Highlands, north of the Great Glen, lies close to the west coast. The long straight valleys of the old rivers run

GLENCOE
Oil painting by Horatio McCulloch, 1864

down to the east. From Strath Conon to Glen Moriston there are a series of the finest glens in the Highlands. With their wealth of birch and tumbling waters they are half-way between the bleakness of the west and the profusion of Deeside. Between the glens lie massive hills like Mam Soul and Carn Eige rising above Glen Affric to nearly 4,000 feet, deer forest and splendid unfrequented walking country. The long glens like Strath Oykell and Strath Bran form the lines of communication from east to west : it is an unforgettable experience to climb slowly up one of these glens to the watershed and then to drop suddenly to the western sea, into a different world, an enchanted land. In the west, the sea and the coast are an essential part of the mountain scene. The hills rise steep out of the submerged valleys, looking every inch their height. Each sea loch is dominated by the mountains at its head—Loch Broom by Ben Dearg, Loch Torridon by Liathac, Loch Duich by the Five Sisters of Kintail, but above all Loch Scavaig in Skye overshadowed by the Cuillin.

The Isles differ little from the mainland. They are the hills which the sea happens to have surrounded. Skye has all the best of the west coast— the dramatically indented coast line, the sea cliffs, the fantastic caves and pinnacles, the brilliant patches of green of the crofting townships, the fairyland views of the other islands, the sweeping panorama of the mainland hills, the soft ever-changing light of the west, the quiet courteous Gaelic-speaking people, the wealth of association from the Vikings to Flora

Macdonald, the variety of bird life, the seals and the basking sharks, the sea-trout—and the rain. These glories it shares with two hundred miles of coast and island from Cape Wrath to the Clyde.

But Skye alone has the Cuillin. In the south-west of the Island there is a tiny group of hills, less than ten miles across in any direction, only just rising to 3,000 feet above the sea. But what a group of hills! The Black Cuillin, dramatically contrasted with the rounded outlines of the Red Cuillin, are a continuous curving ridge of shattered black gabbro, hard, jagged and rough—incomparably the grandest hills in Britain.

The scenery of the west coast really extends along the north coast by Ben Hope to Tongue. I remember vividly the Kyle of Tongue one mid-summer evening. I was with a naturalist. We were on bicycles, and a breeding redwing in full song, the hospitality of the owner of the tree in which it sang and a series of punctures had delayed us. We reached the ferry after midnight by the clock, wondering how we could cross the Kyle at that hour, to find the ferryman and his family sitting out on the grass talking and milking the cows. It was a peaceful cloudless evening, still broad daylight. As we rowed over, the tide was running gently out and the lovely triple crown of Ben Loyal was reflected blue in the loch, while terns flew round us wheeling in formation like a flock of waders.

Wales, like the Highlands of Scotland, is a land of mountains to which a Celtic people withdrew before the invader and in which it has been able to maintain a racial and cultural independence. It was in the mountains of North Wales that Owen Glendower rallied his people and it is to the mountains that they owe their independence. Traditionally they are a hardy pastoral people, poetical, musical and loving their native soil. The mountains are in their blood and when the lure of the coal drew the sons of the hills to the mines of South Wales they continued to show in literature and song an intense nostalgia for their native mountains.

The mountains of Snowdonia are split by main roads into three principal groups—the Glyders, the more gently contoured Carnedds and Snowdon itself (the Welsh y Wyddfa) with its satellites Crib Goch and Lliwedd. On these roads motor traffic penetrates to the heart of the mountains. All my early visits to Wales were spent either at Pen-y-Pass, the little inn at the head of the Pass of Llanberis, or at Helyg, the climbers' hut high up on the Holyhead road. Both these places are well above the tree line. Walking and climbing all day without seeing a tree, I got the impression that it was a country of bold and rugged hills, built on a magnificent scale, but bleak, and uniform in character. I missed the dazzling variety and the friendly valleys of the Lake District. It was not till years later, when I made the acquaintance of the Welsh valleys, that I learnt how wrong I had been.

It was on such expeditions as an ascent of Snowdon from Portmadoc that I discovered that these hills are as richly varied as any. It is a journey

12

VIEW FROM SNOWDON
Water colour by J. Warwick Smith, 1749-1831

of vivid contrasts. From the road which skirts the shore of the reclaimed estuary of the Traeth the distant views of the mountains are tremendous. It makes straight for an apparently impenetrable barrier of rugged bracken- and heather-covered hills ; but at the last moment the gorge of Aber Glaslyn appears, where road, river and railway squeeze miraculously between wooded precipices, to emerge into another world at Beddgelert, lying in its green, mountain-surrounded hollow. From Beddgelert the road con-tinues up Nant Gwynant, a valley of fascinating variety of incident, with views over Llyn Dinas of the land of hidden lakes and valleys which lie round Cnicht. Just short of Llyn Gwynant, loveliest of Welsh lakes, a steep hill track, the Watkin Path, leaves the road for Snowdon. First it follows a bewitching mountain stream which tumbles sparkling from one trans-parent blue rock pool to the next ; across a bare open cwm lying under the flank of Snowdon ; and up on to the rim of the "Horseshoe" to see rock-bound Glaslyn and Llyn Llydaw lying map-like below ; on the right are the cliffs of Lliwedd and to the left the steep zig-zags to the top ; and then the view—with luck Ireland and Scafell.

But it must be admitted that the summit of Snowdon can be a sad anticlimax on a day when the railway brings thousands of trippers to the

13

top. On the other hand, after cutting steps for hundreds of feet up the snow and ice of one of the northern gullies, I have struggled on to the top in a blizzard which has made it seem the wildest place in the world.

The great ridge walks, like the famous Snowdon Horseshoe with the exhilarating stretch along the pinnacles of Crib Goch, are one of the great joys of these hills. From Ogwen there is an expedition even finer than the Horseshoe—from the head of the lake up the north ridge of Tryfan, with plenty of scrambling up the shattered pile of rocks which form this amazing mountain ; down to Bwlch Tryfan and up the Bristly Ridge, by a fascinating route which threads a series of bristling rock pinnacles to the top of Glyder Fach, the strange pile of cromlech-like rocks on which Pennant posed for his portrait; round the shoulder of Glyder Fawr and down by the Gribin, another fine rocky ridge, back to Ogwen. A feature of these Welsh mountain walks is the constant views of the great rock faces, beloved of the rock-climbers.

Everywhere these hills maintain their mountainous scale. Snowdon seen from Capel Curig forms the climax of a real mountain group. From the west side of the Pass of Llanberis the cliffs rise with alpine magnificence. A glimpse of the pinnacles of Crib Goch, red in the sun, high above these shadowed cliffs, makes the heart miss a beat, as does the shimmer of ice suspended above an alpine valley.

From Snowdon the receding ridges of innumerable hills stretch to the Bristol Channel—an endless source of joy for the hill walker. The Arenigs, the Rhinogs and the Arans lying south of Snowdon are all fine shapely hills inviting the mountaineer. But the queen of this mountain-land is Cader Idris. Her craggy summit rises royally from the rich wooded banks of the Mawddach estuary, where the sea enters into the mountain scene as it does in the Western Highlands—but how lavish a scene compared with the treeless sea-lochs of the north. Separated from Cader by the Dovey valley is the vast upland of which Plinlimmon is the highest point. It is strangely thrilling to climb out of one of the romantic tree-filled ravines above Machynlleth, such as the Llyfnant valley, to emerge suddenly on to the barren immensity of the Plinlimmon plateau. Between Plinlimmon and the Bristol Channel lies the massif of the Black Mountains and the Brecon Beacons, from which the deep tragic valleys run down to Newport and Cardiff.

The Lake District is a tiny group of lakes and mountains, separated from the broader masses of the Pennines by the wide fertile red-soiled valley of the Eden. An active walker can cross the whole group in any direction in a day. The configuration of its radiating valleys, eight of which start from within two miles of Styhead tarn, is easy to grasp. In the Highlands there are 276 separate tops over 3,000 feet high ; in the Lakes four. There is something about this quality of smallness and compactness which makes people feel possessive towards these hills.

THE SUMMIT OF SNOWDON, 1852
Water colour by Thomas Miles Richardson the younger, 1813-1890

The Lake District is a part of England no more independent than Cornwall or the Fens. It was too small and too accessible to form a highland retreat for the Celtic population. The dalesmen of the Lake District are by origin and in speech similar to the men of the Pennine dales. They are a slow-spoken friendly people who have for generations practised their traditional and specialised Herdwick sheep farming ; and everywhere the fells and the dales bear witness to this. In recent years dispensing their natural hospitality has become a second industry. There is hardly a farm which does not receive visitors to its hearth with a real North Country welcome. Slate-quarrying comes a poor third to the two main industries.

Here the hills are reduced to the human scale. The fells are so much a part of the dales that as a group of mountains they have not even a name. The district is named after the lakes which lie at their feet ; and the fells often take their names from the farms whose sheep graze over them. In Wales one immediately thinks of the hills as groups divorced from the valleys—the Glyders and the Carnedds ; in the Lake District they are the sides of the valleys—the Langdale Pikes and the Coniston Fells. The fells are not remote from man. From the top of Great Gable one looks straight down on to the jig-saw puzzle of little fields, crooked walls and piles of stones at Wasdale Head. It is never a surprise to meet a fellow man anywhere in these hills. Sheep wander everywhere, and the fells are divided up by an amazing network of dry stone walls. The walled intakes run far up the steep sides of the dales. There is a wealth of old pony-tracks and of well cairned walkers' paths. A Roman road ran along one of the summit ridges. High up on the cliffs of Great Gable is the stone shelter, which may have been a smugglers' retreat. The fell packs, followed on foot by the descendants of John Peel "in his coat so grey," hunt the fox over the roughest hillsides. In fact it is a land of man and the works of his hand.

But as in all hills man has to contend with the weather. It can be as relentless as it can be kind. It can rain with a persistence that I have met nowhere else. The meagre crop of hay is yearly soaked before it can be gathered in. Floods are frequent, sometimes covering the hard-won fields with rocks and debris. In winter many sheep are lost in snow-drifts. On the slopes to the north of Saddleback I have experienced those bewildering conditions when heavy snow is falling on a featureless white blanket, so that sky and earth become merged in one haze, where a man's eye has nothing to focus on but his own footprints. I have climbed on Scafell in conditions as alpine as on Ben Nevis or Snowdon. The weather has the fickleness of the west, and may change in a few moments from sunshine to all-enveloping mist.

Geologically the Lakeland fells divide into three main groups of very different character. In the north the smooth rounded shapes of Skiddaw, Saddleback and Grasmoor are typical of the Skiddaw Slates, comparatively soft rocks, weathering easily and forming long loose screes but few cliffs. Helvellyn, the Langdale Pikes, Scafell, Great Gable, Pillar Fell and all the central hills are carved from the igneous rocks of the Borrowdale Series which have split and weathered into large jagged lumps and form all the finest crags in the district. To the south the Silurian rocks form the gentler wooded hills which surround Windermere and Coniston.

Although the most striking contrasts in scenery are between these different groups, there is an endless variety within each group. The four valleys, for instance, which radiate from Great Gable—Borrowdale, Wasdale, Ennerdale and Buttermere—are of strikingly different character. Borrowdale, above Castle Crag and the wildly romantic Jaws of Borrowdale, is a typical Cumberland dale. On its flat valley bottom are a group of famous sheep farms. Of these Thorneythwaite, with its low line of whitewashed slate-roofed dwellings facing the dry-stone farm buildings and the group of sycamores to provide shade for the clipping, is characteristic of all the dale farms. It differs little from those seen by Francis Towne and his contemporaries, when they came to the Lakes at the end of the eighteenth century to see the balance between untamed nature and the works of man more perfectly adjusted than they have been before or since. The sides of the valley, too, clothed with scrubby birch, oak and ash, and laced with becks which multiply with rain into innumerable milky streaks, have

RAVEN CRAG AND PART OF THIRLMERE

Water colour by Francis Towne, 1740 - 1816

QUINAG FROM UNAPOOL, SUTHERLAND

Coloured lithograph by William Daniell from Ayton's *Voyage Round Great Britain*, 1820

changed little in the last two hundred years. Only the widened roads and a few incongruous buildings have altered the scene.

Wasdale is the grimmest of the genial dales. Its little group of buildings and stone-walled fields lie in a deep trench between the crags of Great Gable and Scafell. The Screes descend so abruptly into Wastwater that they clearly suggest its great depth. Ennerdale, before it was marred by the hapless attempt at afforestation with regimented conifers, shared with Langstrath the honour of being the wildest and most deserted of the dales. The extreme head of the valley remains a fascinating wilderness of hummocky bent-covered moraines, dominated by Gable Crag and the bastion of the Pillar Rock. Buttermere with its tree-fringed lake is the friendliest of these valleys. But I cannot write dispassionately of Buttermere; as a boy most of my holidays were spent there and it is surrounded with an aura of romance which makes it an enchanted valley. The smell of fresh bracken, the noise of rain-lashed windows, bilberry-stained fingers and a thousand other associations common to any hills instantly transport me to Buttermere.

The heads of these four valleys can be linked in a comparatively easy walk by the "Four Passes"—Styhead, Black Sail, Scarth Gap and Honister. The walks on the tops, with, if it is clear, ever changing views from Criffel to Ingleborough and from Cross Fell to the Isle of Man, are perhaps more stirring than those through valley and pass. But the chief delight of Lakeland walking is not in valley walks nor in ridge walks, but in the infinite combinations of the two, in particular those expeditions which lead from the more frequented richer valleys of the early tourists—Grasmere, Rydal and Derwentwater—to the wilder magnificence of the Duddon, the Esk and Wasdale Head.

There is no particular season for the British hills. They are lovely at any time of the year. The Lake District is least attractive in August, when the hills are clothed in a more uniform green than at other seasons, when the weather is generally wet, the flowers are few, the birds have stopped singing and it is hard to find solitude. The brilliance of spring, when the fresh birch and larch are set against the deep brown of the heather and the golden red of last year's bracken, and the panoply of autumn make the valleys as desirable as the summits. But in many ways the winter is loveliest of all, when the landscape becomes a pattern of white and brown, with blue distances and patches of green only in the dales. To have skated on Derwentwater on a fine January morning is an imperishable experience—the snow on the hills, the clear blue of the winter sky, the rime on the trees of shore and island sparkling in the sun, the moving pattern of the skaters and the intoxicating ring of the skates on the creaking ice.

These briefly are the hill districts which aspire to the character of mountains, where the inhabitants are mountain people making their living from the hills. But they are by no means the only hills. There are fine hills

SKIDDAW AND SADDLEBACK
Water colour by Thomas Girtin, 1775-1802

in the Lowlands of Scotland. The Ochil, the Sidlaw and the Lomond Hills, lying between the Highlands and the Firth of Forth, have a particular place in the affections of many Lowlanders. They are chiefly remarkable for their sweeping views of the Highland hills and over the Central Lowlands. A range of hills, known collectively as the Southern Uplands, stretches from sea to sea across the south of Scotland. They are mostly dull and rounded in outline ; and though there is splendid walking to be had on their moorland tops their chief beauty is in such valleys as that of the Esk. A northern spur, the Pentlands, brings mountain scenery almost into Edinburgh, where Arthur's Seat, itself a mountain in miniature, rises from the city roofs. The so-called Ice Cauldron of Galloway and Criffel, I know only from the adventures of Buchan's Richard Hannay and as a distant prospect from the Lake District.

Along the Border, but principally on the English side, lie the Cheviots. Like the Southern Uplands which they resemble, their beauty is not so much in the dreary peat-hags of their tops, but in their deep-cut winding valleys, like those of the Coquet, the Usway and the College Burn. But the special charm of the Middle Marches is in their splendid wildness. One feels that on dark nights the Moss Troopers may still ride. Nowhere is this wildness more keenly appreciated than from Winshields, the highest point on the Roman Wall. Here a land of civilisation—green fields, trees, roads and farmsteads—sweeps up from the south Tyne to stop abruptly at the top of the line of basalt cliffs where Hadrian built his wall looking north over an endless featureless waste of bent and heather, as bleak to-day as it must have been to the shivering legionaries.

VIEW FROM THE SUMMIT OF SCAFELL PIKE
Water colour by William Turner of Oxford, 1841

The greatest upland area in England is the Pennines, running from the Tyne Gap to Dovedale one hundred and fifty miles to the south. The projected Pennine Way from Wooler, on the north-east of the Cheviot, to Edale, just south of the Peak, would give two hundred and fifty miles of continuous hill walking. Cross Fell, the highest point on this route, looks straight across the valley of the Eden to the Lakeland Fells. It is a wonderful view, and on rare occasions, when there is a sea of clouds in the valley and there is snow on Helvellyn, it is miraculous. For those who love the Yorkshire Dales there is no comparable scenery. But again it is the dales with their dignified stone-built farms and villages that attract rather than the remoter appeal of the wind-swept moorland heights. In the neighbourhood of the three Yorkshire giants—Whernside, Ingleborough and Penyghent—a weird interest is introduced into the scene by the dramatic limestone cliffs and chasms, such as Malham Cove and Gordale Scar—the outward and visible signs of the strange underworld of Gaping Gill, Alum Pot and the hundreds of other subterranean water-ways that honeycomb the hillsides. Further south, in the West Riding and Lancashire, the dark satanic mills have crept up the valleys and desecrated the hills. But the Peak District which forms the southern end of the Pennines is another splendid stretch of wild and hilly country. Here there is a striking difference in character between the table-topped gritstone moorland of the "Dark Peak," with its black rocky escarpments and the fantastic limestone rocks and lovely dales of the "White Peak."

Exmoor and particularly Dartmoor have a mountainous character. The steep-sided valleys round the edges and the bleak heathery heights and

19

rocky tors of Dartmoor are in extraordinary contrast with the surrounding country.

England may not be mountainous, but it is not flat. It is full of hills—the Clevelands and North Yorkshire Moors with their abrupt and dramatic edges ; the Shropshire galaxy—the Wrekin, Wenlock Edge, the Stretton and Clee hills ; Clun and Radnor forest marching with Wales ; Bredon and Malvern ; the spectacular limestone scenery of Cheddar Gorge and the Mendips ; the Cotswolds concealing the glory of their stone villages in deep friendly valleys ; Leith Hill and the Forest Ridges rising proudly from the Weald. Each has its own particular beauty ; each in some way echoes the splendour of the greater hills. But the crowning glory of the South Country is the chalk hills, the rolling Downs. They borrow nothing from other hills. There is nothing mountainous about them. The sensuous smooth springy quality of the turf is maintained by the sleek well-fed sheep that graze on them ; the rounded wind-trimmed clumps of beech have been grown by man; his farms, his churches and his villages nestle into their folds ; and everywhere the traces of pre-historic man remind us of the long continuity of human contact with the chalk hills. It is humanised landscape at its best.

THE YORKSHIRE MOORS
Water colour by William Jones, 1839-1931

GATESGARTH-DALE (HONISTER HAUSE)
Aquatint after William Gilpin, 1772

THE SHAPING OF THE HILLS

IN the weird and primeval-looking landscape of the extreme north-west
corner of Scotland the geology of the hills is revealed more forcibly
than in any other part of Britain. Grotesque peaks composed of red
Torridonian sandstone, often terminating in a protective cap of dazzling
bright Cambrian quartzite, rise like prehistoric monsters from a treeless
bed of rugged impervious Lewisian gneiss, where every hollow holds a tiny
lake. The fantastic rock towers of Suilven, Stac Polly and Quinag are the
last degradation of the comparatively soft Torridonian sandstone before it
is finally denuded down to the hard gneiss below.

A recent fall of thousands of tons of rock from the north face of Stac
Polly has emphasised the transitory nature of the everlasting hills. The
gneiss of Lewis and the sandstone of Torridon, rocks of strikingly different
characteristics, belong to the pre-Cambrian age. The Cambrian rocks so
called from their occurrence in North Wales probably began to be formed
about 500 million years ago. They are the first to show recognisable signs
of life. For an incomprehensibly vast period of time before that, well over
1,000 million years, the pre-Cambrian rocks were being formed. They
underlie Britain, form the present land surface of the Highlands and appear
in Wales, the Wrekin and the Malvern Hills.

From Cambrian times onwards geologists have deduced a fairly clear consecutive picture of the formation of our hills. The picture begins with a period of about 150 million years when the greater part of Britain was under the sea, and sediments accumulated locally to a depth of several miles. There was sporadic volcanic activity, and it is submarine ashes and lavas of this period which form the bulk of the rocks of Snowdonia and the Central Lake District. The splendid scenery of Scafell and Snowdon has been carved out of these masses of volcanic rock.

Towards the end of the first marine phase, the great series of upheavals of the Caledonian mountain-building period began. An intense horizontal compression acting from south-east to north-west thrust up the land surface—folding, faulting and pushing the crust to give the rocks of our three mountain groups, the Highlands, the Lake District and North Wales, their original shape. The direction of the folding is still seen in the axis of the Grampians and the line of the fault which forms the Great Glen. The forces which built these mountains also changed the nature of much of the rock, converting the earlier shales and volcanic ashes into the fine slates now quarried at Bethesda, Llanberis and Nantlle and the beautiful green slates of Honister and Tilberthwaite.

The Caledonian upheaval raised most of Britain north of the Thames and the Bristol Channel above the sea, so that it formed part of a great northern continent, perhaps continuous from Greenland to Spitsbergen. Conditions became semi-arid with occasional torrential rains scouring the hills and spreading out vast fans of debris over the lowlands to form the conglomerate and sandstone of the Old Red Sandstone period. Between the mountains were lakes inhabited by the earliest fishes. There was again important igneous activity which produced the lavas now forming the highest ground in Britain. The summit mass of Ben Nevis with the magnificent line of cliffs overlooking the corrie at the head of Allt A'mhuillin and the precipices which form the defile of Glencoe are built of igneous rocks of Old Red Sandstone age.

Gradually the sea advanced northwards, depositing in turn, first the Mountain Limestone now seen in the typical limestone scenery of the Pennines and the Mendips—Goredale Scar and Cheddar Gorge—then the Millstone Grit which forms the steep grit escarpments so characteristic of the Peak District, and finally the sandstones and shales of the coal measures, when sweltering forested swamp produced the wealth of carbonaceous matter which in time became coal.

The second marine phase and period of sedimentation ended as the first with a series of upheavals, the Armorican mountain-building movements.

This time the rocks of Devon, South Wales and the Pennines were compressed and folded, as those of the North had been by the Caledonian movements. Britain was once again dry land, an arid plantless country of

LOCH CORISKIN (LOCH CORUISK), ISLE OF SKYE
Steel engraving by Henry le Keux after J. M. W. Turner, 1775-1851

high mountains, deep valleys, salt lakes and desert conditions in which the rocks of the New Red Sandstone period were formed.

Land now extended far to the north and west of Britain; but a fluctuating and shallow sea encroached from the south-east, at one time covering most of England, Wales and parts of Scotland. In this sea were deposited the oolitic limestones which now stretch in a continuous belt of low hills with fine stone villages from the Yorkshire coast through Oxford and the Cotswolds to Portland Bill, and later the chalk which forms the Downs.

In the succeeding Tertiary period most of Britain was once more above the sea and the climate had become warmer, the south of England being inhabited by crocodiles and turtles. At this time there was considerable volcanic activity in the north-west and immense quantities of basaltic lava were poured out on to the land surface in the Hebrides, and north-east Ireland. This activity produced the columnar basalt of the Giant's Causeway and Staffa and the two most dramatic and mountainous groups of hills in Britain, the granite hills of Aran and the gabbro Black Cuillin of Skye. It was not till after this Hebridean episode that the lost continent of Atlantis finally sank beneath the ocean.

For the last time the whole of Britain was raised to dry land by the last of the great mountain-building upheavals, the Alpine movement, which raised the Himalaya, the Caucasus and the Alps. Britain was only on the outskirts of this disturbance, which pushed up the folds of the chalk hills, later to be worn away to leave the Weald between the North and the South Downs.

By the time the climate had deteriorated sufficiently for the formation of glaciers the hills had been eroded roughly into their present shape. Britain was a peninsula off the coast of Europe. The western sea-board was a regular unindented coast where the continental shelf now lies submerged in the Atlantic. The Highlands were traversed by a series of deep river valleys flowing from north-west to south-east to join the Rhine, with shorter more active westward-flowing rivers capturing their head waters. The dome-like upheaval of the Lake District had been eroded into its characteristic star of radiating valleys. The masses of the Welsh mountains had been cut out by a drainage system similar to that existing to-day, though the Severn, which was subsequently diverted by an ice front, then flowed down the valley of the Dee. Gradually an ice sheet spread out from the mountains till it covered most of Britain north of the Thames and the Bristol Channel. On the east coast it joined with the Scandinavian ice cap. During the ice age, geologically speaking only an interlude of perhaps half a million years, there were fluctuations of the sea and intervening warm periods when the hippopotamus and the rhinoceros shared the land with primitive man.

On the whole the ice cap did not much alter the shape of the hills, and it was in the last phases when the glaciers were retreating up the valleys that the ice was most active as an erosive agent. The evidences of glaciation are clearly seen in all our mountain districts, notably in valleys such as Borrowdale and the Nant Francon. The old "V"-shaped water-worn valleys have been cut into the characteristic ice-worn "U" section. They descend in series of steps often deepened above the drop to form a lake. Above them hang coombes, cwms or corries scooped out under the ridges, where tarns, llyns or lochans spill over to the main valley below in cascades such as Lodore and the three Lakeland Sour Milk Ghylls, where the foaming water pours over the rocks like milk thrown away on the farmyard cobbles. Dominating the coombes are the great northern-facing precipices like Scafell, Craig yr Ysfa and Ben Nevis which were plucked back by the last surviving glaciers.

During and after the ice age there were considerable fluctuations in the level of the sea ; notably the submergence of the west coast of Scotland, creating the magical scene of mountain, sea and island, where the waters have invaded the glacial mountain valleys and isolated the western heights to form the Hebridean archipelago ; but above all the final miracle when the sea broke through the land and cut off our island from the continent of Europe.

Since the ice age the hills have been suffering constant erosion and are gradually returning to their water-worn shapes. Lakes have formed behind rock barriers and dams of moraine, which in many cases like Borrowdale or the lower Nant Francon have silted up to form alluvial flats, or like Buttermere and Crummock have been split in two by converging deltas. There have been changes in climate. Forests have come and gone. Changes in vegetation and methods of farming have from time to time altered the texture of the hills. Man has bound the hills with roads and railways. He has pitted their surface in search of minerals ; but only in the vast slate quarries of North Wales has he substantially altered their shape. The old workings for lead and copper and the once famous black-lead mines at Seathwaite have healed, hardly leaving a scar. New lakes have been formed for water and power. Old ones have been dammed, distorted, discoloured and polluted. Electric cables on giant pylons sweep across moor and down. But broadly speaking the hills remain to us as they were left by the ice.

THOMAS PENNANT ON GLYDER FACH
Engraving from Pennant's *Tour in Wales*, 1773

THE DISCOVERY OF THE HILLS

JUST over two hundred years ago, Captain Burt, an intelligent English soldier garrisoned under General Wade in the Highlands, found the hills most of all disagreeable when the heather was in bloom. He contrasted their "stupendous bulk, frightful irregularity, and horrid gloom" with a "poetical mountain, smooth and easy of ascent, cloth'd with a verdant flowery turf where shepherds tend their flocks, sitting under the shade of tall poplars . . . in short, Richmond Hill."

Captain Burt was typical of an age which was just beginning to acquire an appreciation of landscape, but only landscape which conformed with the pictures of the seventeenth-century painters, Poussin and Claude, where azure mountains closed the distant view. He was no doubt familiar with the poetry of Thomson and Dyer which, describing landscape in terms of pictures, was enjoying a considerable vogue.

He describes in his *Letters to his Friend in London* an attempt by some brother officers to scale Ben Nevis. It is not remarkable at this time that they should have failed in a day of fruitless adventure to get to the top of this "monstrous excrescency," but that they should have had any desire to do so.

Before 1750 occasional ascents of the higher hills were made, generally in the service of science. As early as 1618 John Taylor (The Water Poet) crossed the shapely granite cone of Mount Keen from Glenmark to Braemar. In 1639 Thomas Johnson, a notable botanist, collected specimens on the top of Snowdon ; in 1682 Caswell went up it to determine its height, which he got right to within 140 feet ; and in 1697 Halley made another ascent of the highest point of "this horrid spot of hills" to carry out scientific experiments. Skiddaw too was sometimes climbed ; Bishop Nicolson records in his diary for May 20th, 1684, that he and some friends went up it. Defoe in his *Tour thro' the Whole Island of Great Britain* in 1726 satisfied a "Curiosity of no extraordinary kind" by climbing the Great Cheviot. The expedition was made on horseback except for the last few hundred feet which the party worked upon their feet. Defoe who had apprehended that on top they would be "just as upon a pinnacle . . . and . . . should have only room enough to stand, with a precipice every way round" was as agreeably surprised as the walker to-day is disappointed, to find the summit "a most pleasant plain, of at least half a mile in diameter." Science was not neglected, as one of their company, "a good botanist, fell to searching for simples, and, *as he said*, found some nice plants."

But these were exceptional events ; it was not till the second half of the eighteenth century that the "discovery" of the hills began. In the fifties and sixties the new demand on the topographical draughtsmen for landscape views in addition to views of houses and antiquities led them to the Lake District. The publication of Macpherson's controversial "translation"

DR. SYNTAX SKETCHING THE LAKES
Coloured aquatint by Thomas Rowlandson, 1812

of Ossian in 1760-63 gave an impetus to the appreciation of wild and rugged scenery; and the improvement in the roads was making such scenery more accessible. Engravings of drawings such as the Lake District views of Thomas Smith of Derby became familiar in the South. In the fifties, Dr. Dalton of Oxford wrote a Descriptive Poem about the Lakes and Dr. John Brown of Cambridge wrote a letter from Keswick to Lord Lyttleton, both of which seem to have received considerable attention. Amongst Dalton's trite descriptions of "the beauteous brook of Borrowdale" and the "rough rocks of dread Lowdore" there are occasional glimpses of something more than the fashionable couplets and the fashionable adjectives:

> "There the brown fells ascend the sky,
> Below the green enclosures lye;
> Along their sloping sides supine
> The peaceful villages recline:
> On azure roofs bright sunbeams play
> And make the meanest dwellings gay."

To notice the sparkle of the sun on Buttermere green-slate roofs shows a visual perception rare before Dorothy Wordsworth, half a century later, vividly recorded impressions of this sort. Brown in his letter finds the full perfection of Keswick to consist of three circumstances—beauty, horror

27

and immensity ; and to give an idea of them would require the united powers of Claude, Salvator and Poussin. The poem and the letter are the first descriptions of mountainous scenery in the picturesque terms of Dyer and Thomson.

Dalton and Brown were probably responsible for sending Arthur Young and the poet Thomas Gray on their visits to the Lakes, in 1768 and 1769 respectively. In Young's *Tours*—officially treatises on agriculture—his theories on fertilising and stock-breeding, crops and enclosure, are enlivened by descriptions of picture galleries and landscape. He saw the Lakes transformed into a series of pictures by Claude, differing as little as possible from those he had recently seen in some country house. The bleaker scenery of the Yorkshire moors would not conform with classical standards ; they were dreary wastes only to be mitigated by the possibility of reclamation.

In 1765 Gray had visited the Highlands, safe for tourists since the suppression of the clans after the '45, and found the mountains "ecstatic." Four years later in the Lakes he gave himself wholeheartedly to the pursuit of the picturesque. At Keswick he "passed six days lap'd in Elysium." His *Journal* is a sensitive and unpretentious record, and in such observations as "Saddleback, whose furrowed sides were gilt by the noon-day sun, whilst its brow appeared of a sad purple, from the shadow of the clouds as they sailed slowly by it," there is a hint of Wordsworth and the romantic association of mood with landscape. He did not venture deeper into the dales than Grange ; but he made the best of the mysteries he did not investigate. He reported that at the head of Borrowdale all farther access is barred to prying mortals, "only there is a little path winding over the fells, and for some weeks in the year passable to the dalesmen ; but the mountains know well that these innocent people will not reveal the mysteries of their ancient kingdom." Macaulay, not content with Gray's imaginative exaggeration, characteristically improved it into "Even after the accession of George III the path over the fells from Borrowdale to Ravenglass was still a secret carefully kept by the Dalesmen, some of whom had probably in their youth escaped from the pursuit of justice by that road." And this describes the Styhead track which must have been a high road for the dalesmen and their ponies at all seasons of the year.

A much more adventurous and less imaginative mountaineer than Gray was Thomas Pennant, described by Dr. Johnson as the best traveller he ever read. Pennant, Flintshire squire, naturalist, friend of Linnaeus, correspondent of Gilbert White, and amateur archaeologist, was an insatiable traveller and writer. In 1769 and 1772 he explored North Britain, a country "as little known to its Southern Brethren as Kamschatka." He describes the country, the customs and appearance of the natives, the flora and fauna, buildings and objects of antiquarian interest, as an objective explorer and is not troubled with picturesque descriptions of landscape. In Skye he got

SOUTH-WEST PROSPECT OF THE COUNTRY FROM PEELNEARS, CONISTON
Wash drawing by Stephen Penn, 1732

to the top of Beinn na Caillich, one of the red hills behind Broadford, from which he saw the panorama of the Cuillin as a prospect of desolation itself—"a savage series of rude mountains, discoloured black and red, as if by the rage of fire. . . . The serrated tops of *Blaven* affect with astonishment ; and beyond them, the clustered height of *Quillin*, or, the mountain of Cuchullin, like its ancient hero, *stood like a hill that catches the clouds of heaven*." From Loch Broom he penetrated by Cam Loch to Ledbeg under the slopes of Canisp, to-day still one of the remotest corners of Britain. Of the strange landscape between Loch Broom and Loch Assynt he says "I never saw a country that seemed to have been so torn and convulsed : the shock, whenever it happened, shook off all that vegetates : among these aspiring heaps of barrenness, the sugar-loaf hill of *Suil-bhein* made a conspicuous figure : at their feet, the blackness of the moors by no means assisted to chear our ideas." In Wales he ascended most of the principal peaks, recording the details of his climbs with great accuracy. His *Journey to Snowdon* became the source book for many of the early guides to the district.

In his *Journey to the Western Islands of Scotland* in 1773, Dr. Johnson, like Pennant, describes a wild and foreign land inhabited by strange aborigines. His attitude to mountains and wild scenery is, as one would

CADER IDRIS FROM LLANELLTYD
Wash drawing by Cornelius Varley, 1803

expect, the classical view that nature untamed is chaos ; only by the hand of man can she be made beautiful. In Skye he was not interested in those prospects of the Cuillin which leave the modern tourist gasping with admiration.

While Johnson was writing his *Journey*, a shy Hampshire parson, William Gilpin, "the venerable master of the picturesque," was compiling a series of works which formulated a point of view very different from the doctor's Augustan attitude. The original of Rowlandson's and Combe's Dr. Syntax on his grotesquely picturesque white horse, he rode through England, Scotland and Wales in search of picturesque views. He described and catalogued them, propounding simple rules for the selection and arrangement of natural objects to form a suitable composition ; and enumerating appropriate Backgrounds, Offskips and Foregrounds. His books were illustrated by aquatints in monochrome of landscape reduced to its simplest picturesque terms. In the *Observations on the Mountains and Lakes of Cumberland and Westmoreland* there is a diagram illustrating why certain hills including Saddleback are incorrect. His deepest penetration into the mountains was into Gatesgarth-dale (Honister) where "Fruitful nature, making in every part of her ample range, unremitting efforts to vegetate, could not here produce a single germin." Of his illustration of this scene he rightly complains that the figures destroy the scale by being twice as large as they ought to be. In Wales he did not ascend Snowdon and had to

30

CADER IDRIS FROM LLANELLTYD
Drawing continuing the subject on the opposite page

rely on quotations from Pennant's account. His books were immensely popular.

During the last twenty years of the eighteenth century, mountains became the rage. Tourists, fed on Gilpin, Gray and Young, flocked to Llanberis, Loch Lomond and Lodore. The prospect of Snowdon from Llyn Padarn and of Keswick Lake became stock views. Countless guide-books appeared. West's Guide, the first about the Lake District, had run into seven editions by 1799. West worked out stations from which the devotee could be assured of seeing a truly picturesque composition; and, if unable to sketch himself, he could condense and frame the picture in his Claude glass. His stations, together with several others, are marked on the maps of the Lakes surveyed, planned and published from 1783 onwards by "Peter Crosthwaite, Admiral at Keswick Regatta, who keeps the Museum at Keswick, and is Guide, Pilot, Geographer and Hydrographer to the Nobility and Gentry, who make the Tour of the Lakes." Local guides conducted tourists up Snowdon and Skiddaw, both of which could be climbed on a pony. Mrs. Radcliffe recorded her ascent in an account as highly coloured as some of the descriptive passages in *Udolpho*. Occasionally braver spirits would ascend other summits—Saddleback, Helvellyn and the Glyders. By the end of the eighteenth century the fell-walker had appeared. Joseph Budworth in *A Fortnight's Ramble to the Lakes* in 1792 describes the father of all Lake District walking tours, when he and his companion

31

"walked upwards of two hundred and forty miles, besides boat and chaise."
In less than forty years, mountains had passed from being useless obstacles,
to become the height of fashion. "What," cried Elizabeth Bennet, "are
men to rocks and mountains?"

While the poets, the tourists, and the itinerant sketchers were dis-
covering the mountains, the mountains themselves were having a profound
effect on landscape painting.

From the time of the blue distances of the Italians and the weird rock
scenes of the Flemish painter Patinir, mountains as backgrounds were
common in European painting. But mountains alone were not considered
an adequate subject for a picture. There are some early drawings of
the Lake District Fells by Stephen Penn. His prospect of the country
from Peelnears, dated 1732, shows the Coniston Fells carefully delineated,
coloured, numbered and named. But it is a piece of pictorial cartography
rather than a picture; and it was not till well after 1750 that mountain
views began to become popular.

Richard Wilson returned from Rome in 1755 deeply influenced by what
he had seen of Italy and the works of the seventeenth-century painters.
He painted in his own simplified idiom picturesque classical landscape
compositions, rich in quality of paint and suffused with a mellow golden
light, owing much to Claude and Poussin. But when he went back to Wales
he was sufficiently moved by his native mountains to abandon the accepted
tradition and to record his own feelings for the hills. When he climbed to
Llyn Cau to make his studies for the well-known picture of Cader Idris
(reproduced in Rhys Davies' book, *The Story of Wales*, in this series), he left
the picturesque far behind. These pictures, admired by Pennant, are the
first romantic interpretation in paint of the emotional reactions of an artist
to the hills. They remain among the very few really satisfactory mountain
paintings.

Amongst the innumerable topographers who were developing the art
of drawing in water colour in the mountain beauty spots in the second half
of the century a few stand out, such as Paul Sandby and Edward Dayes,
whose drawings of the hills in delicate line and wash are of far more than
topographical interest. But one feels that many of these men went to the
hills because mountain scenes were popular and engravings of them would
sell. With Francis Towne it was very different. He was fascinated by the
structure of mountains. When he first saw them in Wales in 1777 he
remained somewhat aloof. But when he toured the Lakes eleven years later,
with the experience of his remarkable Swiss drawings behind him, the
mountains were the centre of his interest. The actual forms of the hills
are lovingly studied and outlined with sensitive brown pen lines, reminiscent
of the pen and wash landscape drawings of Edward Lear; the masses are
washed in with clear, cold, transparent colour, which in its simplicity of
pattern foreshadows Cotman. At Buttermere, for instance, he did not draw

SPRING IN ESKDALE, SCOTLAND

Oil painting by James McIntosh Patrick, 1935

By courtesy of Messrs. Arthur Tooth & Sons Ltd.

VIEW FROM THE WHITE HART, GUESTLING, SUSSEX

Oil painting by J. D. Innes, c. 1911

the conventional view of the lake but recorded in a long panoramic drawing the detailed structure of the hills from Fleetwith to High Stile. Towne was not interested in dramatic or romantic effects of light and weather. His drawings had no contemporary appeal and were neglected for a hundred years. John "Warwick" Smith, who seems to have studied the hills with the same devotion as his companion, Towne, produced within the limitations of the topographical idiom many hill drawings. Towne's pupil, John White Abbot, visiting the Lakes in 1791, made a series of drawings which might be copies of those of his master.

In Towne's Lake District drawings there is little of the picturesque, and the sublime is tamed out of recognition. "Sublime" was the term popularised by Burke to describe compositions into which the element of agreeable terror was introduced. It described those objects which were covered neither by "Beautiful" nor "Picturesque." The topographical painter to represent the sublime was Philip James de Loutherbourg. He was obsessed with dramatic effects, painted scenery for Garrick and Sheridan, and exhibited his Eidophusikon, a small stage where thunder and lightning broke over a mountain scene, the rising moon was contrasted with the effect of fire on the Mediterranean, and Satan arrayed his troupe on the banks of the Fiery Lake. His *Romantic and Picturesque Scenery of England and Wales* (1805) included a few mountain scenes. In the familiar view of Snowdon the picturesque trees are lashed by the wind and the clouds swirl round the summits like an animated stage effect; and in 'Lynn Ogwen' the precipices of Tryfan are piled above the lake with a sublimity compared with which the magnificence of the actual scene seems tame indeed.

Gilpin explained that his own illustrations of the Lakes made no pretence to being portraits, as Mr. Farington's prints made any other portraits unnecessary. These engravings from drawings by Joseph Farington, from whose diaries so much of our knowledge of artists at the turn of the century is derived, are accurate pictures of the conventional Lake District views, and are typical of the wealth of competent engravings of the hills which were being issued to illustrate the popular guides and tours.

By the beginning of the nineteenth century the reproduction of water-colour drawings in aquatint had become a fine art. Paul Sandby had been an early experimenter; but his mountain prints, such as 'Pont Aber Glaslyn,' are crude compared with his drawings. The high-water mark of the topographical aquatint is the series of three hundred and eight views made by William Daniell for Ayton's *Picturesque Voyage round Great Britain* (1814-25). They are coastal scenes, but he clearly delighted above all in drawing hills which are introduced whenever there is an excuse. The west coast of Scotland, where sea and mountain meet, was his paradise. He was too absorbed in depicting the form of the hills, to allow them to be obscured by clouds. Even when in the Kyle of Lochalsh the sea is animated by a high wind and the busy ships are in full sail, the effect is static and the mountains tranquil.

Contemporary with Daniell's *Voyage* were T. H. Fielding's and J. Walton's forty-eight coloured views for *A Picturesque Tour of the English Lakes*, and *The Scenery of the Grampian Mountains* with forty aquatints from drawings by George Fennell Robson, who made a thorough exploration of the Highlands and also drew Welsh and Lake District scenes. His views are sincere formalised statements of the hills as he saw them. Although his view of Loch Coruisk is strictly topographical, the hard blue silhouette of the Cuillin ridge romantically evokes the qualities of Skye. Robson travelled with a copy of *The Lady of the Lake* in his pocket, and it is not therefore surprising to find him enough the child of fashion to put three fancy-dress figures in the spot where the adventures of Robert the Bruce and Ronald of the Isles in the *Lord of the Isles* reached a climax. The figures in Robson's pictures were sometimes added by Joshua Cristall and the deer by Robert Hills. Cristall's own line drawings show a keen eye for the mountains, but in his more ambitious water colours figures in classical tunics shivering in Borrowdale introduce a curiously artificial atmosphere. Robson's stags and chieftain lead straight to Horatio McCulloch and the romantic glories of Victorian Highland landscape.

With the exception of Wilson it is the water-colour draughtsmen, big men and little men, who have reacted most happily to the hills. The transparent quality of the medium is particularly suited to interpreting the

LOCH CORUISK AND THE CUCHULLIN (CUILLIN) MOUNTAINS, ISLE OF SKYE
Water colour by George Fennell Robson, 1788-1833

TRYFAN AND LLYN OGWEN
Coloured aquatint by Philip James de Loutherbourg, 1805

watery atmosphere of the hills. Rocks have a special appeal for the draughtsman. Crome and Constable, both primarily oil painters, were neither of
them happy in the mountains. John Crome went to the Lakes in 1802 and
1806, teaching drawing to Elizabeth Fry's six sisters, the Gurneys of Earl-
ham. The large oil painting of "The Slate Quarries" in the National
Gallery, an interesting breakaway from the classical picturesque tradition,
is the result of these trips. John Constable was persuaded into going to
the Lakes in the autumn of 1806. Five years earlier he had been in Derby-
shire, where he had made a series of sketches in very pale monochrome,
showing an interest in the form of rocks. In his two months' visit to the
Lakes he wandered about Borrowdale, Thirlmere and Langdale recording
with his usual intense sincerity, in a series of muddy water-colour and
monochrome sketches, his feelings for the hills. He did not choose the
conventional viewpoints, sketching from such places as Styhead and the
fells above Rosthwaite. The drawings are utterly unpicturesque. Unlike his
predecessors he was less interested in the form of the hills than in effects
of light and weather. On the back of the paper he pencilled "twylight
after a very fine day," "dark autumnal day at noon," "evening stormy
with slight rain." But Constable was not happy in the hills and admitted

35

that the solitude of mountains oppressed his spirits. He painted no important picture from the Lake District sketches and never returned to hilly country.

Thomas Girtin loved the grandeur of hills and the broad masses of the Yorkshire dales. His few mountain drawings such as those made round about Beddgelert in 1800 and his view of Skiddaw and Saddleback are tantalising reminders of what might have come had he lived longer. John Sell Cotman may have met Girtin in Wales when he too was being carried away by the mountains and lakes. Though he never returned to the hills after his two early visits to Wales in 1800 and 1802, he drew on his Welsh sketches and memories for the rest of his life. When he made his alternative version of 'Greta Bridge,' either nostalgia for the hills or a desire to be more fashionable made him substitute mountains for clouds ; and more than thirty years later when he was attempting to achieve the brilliance of oils by painting in the coloured scum collected off fermenting paste, he returned to the inspiration of Wales for his pictures of intensely blue mountains and rich brown foregrounds.

Of Cotman's contemporaries, David Cox and the Varley brothers were devoted to the mountains of Wales. John Varley's output was immense and uneven. The best of his earlier drawings of the hills have much in common with the broad and sober washes of Girtin and Cotman. The pencil and wash drawings of Cader Idris from Llanelltyd, by his less ambitious brother Cornelius, are beautiful pieces of straightforward sensitive draughtsmanship. Many of John Varley's innumerable pupils painted mountain scenes. William Turner of Oxford, for instance, after visiting Loch Duich and Skye in 1838 abandoned pastoral landscape and the Thames for the hills. His highly accurate drawing of the view from the top of Scafell Pike, on the back of which he has inscribed Dorothy Wordsworth's description of the scene, is a fascinating piece of painstaking observation.

Nature, particularly as displayed in mountains and the sea, was the inspiration of J. M. W. Turner's bewildering virtuosity. From 1795 onwards he dashed through the Lake District, Wales, Scotland and the Alps, filling sketch-book after sketch-book with notes of hill, river and lake and seeing in them aspects of nature which no one before had dreamed of. Starting, with Girtin, as a highly skilled topographical draughtsman, he soon forsook topography for wildly romantic visions of storm and sunshine. The mountains were flooded with lowering clouds and shafts of light. In the drawing of Loch Corriskin (Coruisk), engraved for his illustrations of *The Lord of the Isles*, mountains and mist swirl in one great vortex, like Leonardo's drawings of the deluge. In his later drawings the hills were finally drowned in a shimmer of luminous colour.

Turner's visions of the hills coincide with Scott and Wordsworth. Like Turner's early topographical drawings, reaching beyond the picturesque

KIRKSTONE PASS IN A SNOW-STORM
Coloured aquatint by T. H. Fielding, 1821

to a more romantic view of nature, but still traditional in form, Scott's descriptions of wild and mountainous scenery found a receptive public. *The Lady of the Lake* and *The Lord of the Isles* were read in every polite home. The Waverley novels enjoyed a remarkable popularity. When Frank Osbaldistone in *Rob Roy* approached the bleak Northumbrian moors and frowning majesty of the Cheviots with "that enthusiasm which romantic and wild scenery inspires in lovers of nature," no one pointed out the anachronism. But the scene is set a century and a half before the Brontës reacted to the magic of the moors. Scott saw nature as part of personal experience and not, like Mrs. Radcliffe, as a picture in a frame.

In 1799 at the height of the Lake District boom, William Wordsworth, already a lover of the fells by birth and upbringing, settled at Grasmere, in which neighbourhood he lived till his death in 1850. At a time when the "Lakers" rarely ventured beyond Lodore, Wordsworth wandered freely among the "fraternal hills," absorbing the inspiration of their changing moods, so that he could interpret to man the spiritual message of the mountains. When the servant-maid at Rydal Mount told a visitor that her master's study was in the fields, she unwittingly hit upon the chief source

37

of his inspiration. Wordsworth's mountain poetry, with its new philosophy of nature, must have been strangely moving when it first appeared; but now much of it is less evocative than the simple sparkling prose of his sister Dorothy. William's "dread chasms," "airy summits," "green dales," "limpid waters" and "glorious morns" are dead compared with Dorothy's "The sky was clear and blue ; and light and shade fell in masses upon the mountains, the fields below *glittered* with the dew, where the beams of the sun could reach them, and every little stream tumbling down the hills seemed to add to the chearfulness of the scene" from her account of her excursion up Scafell in 1818.

Wordsworth's *Guide to the Lakes* is full of fine descriptive prose and good sense about the nature and "preservation" of the Lake Country. Matthew Arnold's story of the clergyman who asked Wordsworth if he had written anything else gives us an idea of the importance of the book in some quarters.

To-day the shadow of the Lake Poets hangs heavy over Grasmere and Derwentwater ; Dove Cottage is a museum ; and stained-glass windows in the Keswick hotels depict Coleridge, Southey and Wordsworth. But the romantic associations of the Lakes are nothing to those of the Highlands. Ronald of the Isles and Ellen Douglas, Waverley and Rob Roy moving through Scott's pages in fancy dress are symptoms of an astonishing change in attitude of Lowlanders on both sides of the Border to the High-landers. In little more than a generation the marauding cut-throats from the mountains became objects of an exaggerated romantic admiration. Plaids and claymores, pipes and kilts became the rage. The King of England appeared at Holyrood disguised (to quote Macaulay) "in what before the Union was considered by nine Scotchmen out of ten as the dress of a thief." *La Sylphide* was danced in London in Highland costume. At Balmoral the walls and the floors were covered with special tartans, devised by the Queen and Consort ; and beautifully designed Highland figures supported the lights. The 'Monarch of the Glen' proudly surveyed southern drawing-rooms, while his living counterpart was pursued in northern corries by kilted Englishmen.

The cult of Highland associations still flourishes. For many the glories of the Bens and the Glens are intensified by memories of the wanderings of Prince Charlie and David Balfour ; Ossianic myths of Fingal and Cuchu-lainn add romance to the Hebrides; and the charge of the clans at Killie-crankie, the massacre of the Macdonalds at Glencoe, and the betrayal of Montrose at Ardvreck lend tragic glamour to scenes in themselves sublime.

But, if it is hard to escape tartan ribbon and Highland cattle in Princes Street and stained-glass Lake Poets in Keswick, it is at least easy to do so in the hills themselves. In our ability to enjoy their beauties we unconscious-ly inherit so much from the picturesque travellers and the romantics, that there is no need for the stimulus of an artificial romanticism.

EAST FACE OF KERN KNOTTS, GREAT GABLE
Pencil drawing by W. Heaton Cooper, 1936

THE CLIMBING OF THE HILLS

A MOTORIST travelling along the main London-Holyhead road on any fine summer day will witness, as he approaches the tenth milestone from Bangor, a most remarkable sight. As he turns the corner at the head of Llyn Ogwen, where the crags of Tryfan sweep down to the head of the lake, he will see a hundred yards or so above the road a bold

39

buttress of rock, covered with a motley collection of men and women, weaving weird patterns over the rocks with ropes. Some will be happily poised on perilous-looking slabs of stone ; others struggling in obvious agony in cruel-looking cracks and crannies. Strange snatches of technical jargon will echo down to him on the road. This is the "Milestone Buttress," the most accessible of British rock-climbs ; and these are the devotees of a popular sport enjoying their peculiar pleasures.

It is interesting to trace the changes which have led from the days when men diffidently approached the crags in a spirit of scientific enquiry, or viewed them from afar as picturesque incidents in the landscape, to these days when the Pillar Rock, the ridges of Tryfan, the face of Scafell, the Cuillin of Skye and innumerable other cliffs have become a happy hunting-ground for thousands of climbers.

It is not necessary to be able to climb rocks to reach any of the summits on the mainland of Britain. But anyone walking in the hills soon finds that his freedom is restricted if he cannot readily scramble up and down barriers of rock. This limitation was brought home to the early tourists by the difficulties of getting from Scafell Pike to Scafell. "The two summits," wrote Harriet Martineau in 1854, "are about three-quarters of a mile apart, in a straight line ; but the great chasm between them, called Mickledore, renders a wide circuit necessary. There have been foolhardy persons who have passed Mickledore without losing their lives ; and there are strangers, almost every season, who attempt the ascent without a guide. These last usually pay the penalty of their rashness in hours of uneasy wandering and excessive fatigue." The route which the foolhardy followed to get from Mickledore to the top of Scafell, known as the Broad Stand, is a steep little rock-climb involving some scrambling and one awkward pull-up over a vertical wall. It had long been known to shepherds, and Coleridge who was a more adventurous fell-walker than most of his contemporaries probably descended by it. If so, he was one of the earliest English rock-climbers.

The first recorded rock-climb in Britain was the ascent by a dalesman in 1826 of the Pillar Rock, the great tower which stands detached from the side of the fell high over Ennerdale. His feat which got great publicity at the time was only repeated six times before 1850 ; and generally speaking natives and visitors alike were content to leave the rocks alone. During these years scientific exploration had introduced the early mountaineers to the joys of climbing in the Alps ; and by the fifties mountaineering had become a sport to be enjoyed for its own pleasures and excitements without any ulterior motives. For the next thirty years Englishmen climbing with skilled peasant guides swept all before them in the Alps, making the first ascents of most of the peaks in the "Playground of Europe."

At home, particularly in winter and spring, these men would occasionally take holidays in the hills, which they treated as a practice ground for the

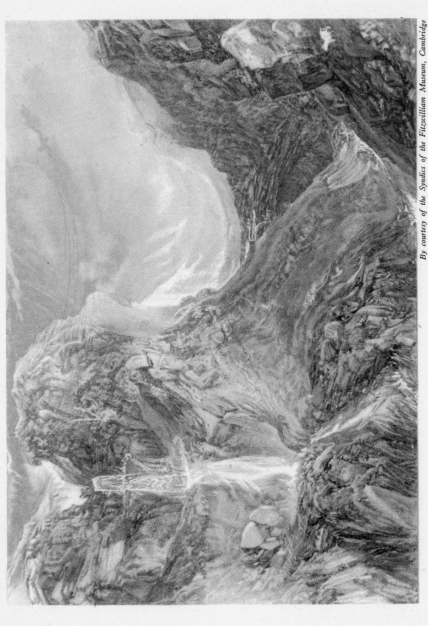

MOSSDALE FALL, NEAR HAWES, YORKSHIRE

Water colour by J. M. W. Turner, 1775 - 1851

CUL MOR, STAC POLLY, CUL BEAG AND BENN AN EOIN IN THE WESTERN HIGHLANDS

STAC POLLY, BENN AN EOIN, SUILVEN, QUINAG, CUL MOR AND CUL BEAG

Pen and water colour sketches by Peter Bicknell, 1943

Alps. They tramped the ridges and scrambled up easy rocks and snow-filled gullies. As in the Alps they reached the tops by the most obvious and easy routes. They practised the same elementary method of climbing rocks which was all that was required on the classical alpine routes. In Skye, in particular, where there were still virgin peaks to be climbed, they found expeditions which reminded them most closely of the ridges with which they were familiar abroad.

But it was not just members of the Alpine Club with the means and the time for holidays in Switzerland, who began to discover the joys of climbing in the hills at home. In the Lake District, a vigorous school of local climbers were the forerunners of thousands of men and women who have since discovered for themselves the recreative adventure of scrambling and climbing on the rocks and ridges of their native hills.

By 1880 all the great Alpine peaks had been climbed and enterprising mountaineers turned their attentions to alternative routes and subsidiary summits of greater technical difficulty. The consequent advance in Alpine rock-climbing skill was soon reflected in Britain. In the eighties and nineties cragsmen at home began to explore the great rock faces for their own sake. At first the insistence was on climbs with some definite point in view, such as the Pillar, the Napes Needle and Scafell Pinnacle. But as technique improved and progressively more difficult routes were attempted the climbers became more and more absorbed in the routes themselves.

The history of rock-climbing since it became a sport in its own right is one of increasing skill. When the easy way was abandoned for more artificial routes which were not necessarily the simplest way to the top of the crags the climbers first took to the clefts in the rock where the enclosing walls gave a reassuring sense of security. Struggling to overcome gravity in a confined space they evolved a gymnastic type of climbing where body, arms and legs all wrestled with the resistant and often soaking or slimy rock. The first ascents of such climbs as the Water Pipe Gully in Skye, the Great Gully on Craig yr Ysfa and Moss Ghyll on Scafell, all of which are great clefts which split a cliff from top to bottom, were heroic achievements. But a gully is apt to be a waterfall when it rains and even in fine weather is a dark and sunless place. As self-confidence grew climbers ventured on to the ridges which separated the gullies. On Tryfan, and the Napes of Great Gable they were familiar with buttresses of rock where their gymnastic technique could be employed in heaving the body from one good hold to the next by the instinctive method of grip and pull common to men and monkeys. Gradually they discovered that if the weight is placed vertically over the foot a very small hold will suffice for safety. The hands are needed for balance but great muscular exertion is not required. Hitherto, the cliffs of the East Peak of Lliwedd, near Snowdon, had been considered impracticable, as the vertical ribbed structure of the rock yields no clean-cut holds for the hands. On this cliff a small group of

41

enthusiasts worked out the new technique of balanced climbing, in a series of steep and exposed routes. By 1914 rock-climbing had passed through the growing-pain stage ; and climbers were moving easily and safely over slabs which a short time before had appeared holdless.

After the Armistice, when foreign travel was difficult and expensive, and motors made it easy to reach the hills, rock-climbing began to enjoy an unprecedented popularity. Hundreds of climbers took to the crags, climbing the old routes till they became branded and polished by boot nails, and working out endless new routes and variations. Climbing clubs were active, providing cheap shelter in mountain huts and sound training for their members ; the routes old and new were catalogued, classified and minutely described in guides issued by the clubs. The gritstone edges of the Pennines, the Cornish sea-cliffs, even rocks near Tunbridge Wells and the buildings of Oxford and Cambridge became practice grounds. Newcomers to the hills, standing on the shoulders of their predecessors, often acquired in a few weeks the skill that it had taken previous generations half a century to perfect.

Steadily the skill of the experts increased. The general use of rubber shoes in fine weather made possible places unclimbable in the traditional nailed boots. One guide-book even inveighed against the practice of climbing a "rubber" climb of filigree delicacy in boots.

Meanwhile the art of safeguarding the climber had kept pace with the increased difficulty of the climbs. Until the eighties a rope was not generally used on British rocks. But from the elementary rope technique of the early Alpine mountaineers, a system has been perfected by which every member of the party, except occasionally the leader, is completely safe. Much thought has gone into the organisation of rescue operations for climbers and walkers who do get into trouble. And to co-ordinate and represent the common interests of the various rock-climbing and mountaineering clubs a British Mountaineering Council was formed in 1944.

In the late twenties and early thirties a school of brilliant young rock-climbers had emerged who climbed places of incredible difficulty with an ease and grace which would have astonished the giants of the past. With one exception all the major rock faces had been climbed and explored before 1914, so that the efforts of the inter-war climbers were directed to new facets of old rocks and to minor crags. The one exception was Clogwyn du'r Arddu. Anyone who has gone up Snowdon from Llanberis on a clear day, either on foot or in the train, is familiar with the tremendous wall of rock that stands on his right during most of the ascent. From the climbing point of view it is the most forbidding of all British crags. Early climbers had nibbled at its edges, but it had been written off as unclimbable. A writer had suggested that there was one line of ascent which offered the faintest of faint hopes for a human fly. The cliff is split in two by a steep but easy terrace. A route was made up the left-hand half of the cliff in 1927.

It was a splendid climb, but left the grander half of the cliff, the West Buttress, still untouched. In the following year I was lucky enough to watch a human fly make his way up the West Buttress.

A small party had gathered at Pen-y-Pass at Whitsun hoping to make an assault. Two of the party had already made an extensive reconnaissance of the climb and our hopes ran high. We were not much disturbed by rumours of climbers having been seen on the West Buttress the previous day. But as we came in sight of the rocks, to our undisguised disappointment we saw a party established on the bottom of the climb. We walked on to the foot of the cliff discussing alternative plans. But then occurred one of those picturesque incidents which still occasionally take place on battlefields and in the jungle. The climbers, recognising our party, came down, and with a "Your climb, Sirs," prepared to withdraw. After a short discussion, however, they agreed to form a combined party to be conducted by our leader. We, the spectators, sat in the sun and bathed in the lake at the foot of the cliff, watching with fascination the steady progress of the party up the rocks. The climb is spectacular, the greater part of it going up a vicious sloping slab leaning out over an overhang. At the top of this slab there is a particularly steep final section leading on to a tiny ledge which might well have been impossible. As the leader proceeded up the slab thunder clouds were gathering and it became obvious that there was going to be a heavy storm. If it began to rain before he reached the shelf, his position in rubber shoes might be precarious. He pulled himself on to it just as the heavens opened, and our cheers were drowned by the thunder and the hiss of the rain on the rocks. The apparently overhanging wall above the ledge seemed to offer no difficulties, and four and a half hours after they had started we watched the party completing in heavy rain as fine a bit of climbing as anyone is likely to witness.

Since then many climbs of even greater technical difficulty have been achieved, and there seems no end to what may become possible.

The growing popularity of climbing has only been part of a larger movement—the discovery of the hills by the masses—itself an offshoot of the general increase in open-air activities. Rock-climbing has long since become a sport as divorced from mountaineering as down-hill ski-racing is from mountain travel. The walker who can find his way safely over Helvellyn or the Glyders in bad weather is far more of a mountaineer than the rock expert who can lead a party up Clogwyn du'r Arddu on a fine day. But it is those who can do both that are equipped to get the fullest pleasure from the hills.

LAKELAND FARM, AMBLESIDE, AT THE HEAD OF WINDERMERE
Water colour by Francis Towne, 1786

THE FUTURE OF THE HILLS

NOW another war is over and everything from holidays with pay to difficulties of foreign travel is conspiring to flood the hills with swarms of holiday-makers, many problems which have been simmering for years must come to the boil.

Recent tragedies have emphasised the importance of newcomers finding out how to look after themselves in the hills. Ignorance of elementary precautions has often led to death, and time and time again has caused needless toil and anxiety for dwellers in the valleys, whose lives are busy enough without searching the hills for foolish visitors.

Great Britain is one of the few countries where the public has not the legal right to wander over the hills. There is a tradition of free access to the Lake District Fells and North Wales ; but from other districts, notably the Peak and great tracts of mountain in Scotland, visitors have been rigorously excluded. In the past access has been denied, at any rate during some seasons of the year, to about four and a half million acres of grouse moor and over three and a quarter million acres of deer forest. The vast army of town dwellers who live round the fringes of the Peak District have particularly resented their exclusion from their natural playground, in order that a limited number of sportsmen should enjoy record bags of grouse on a few days during the year. In 1932 guerilla warfare broke into an open battle on Kinder between hikers and keepers supported by the police, which resulted in sentences amounting to seventeen months being passed on six of the victims.

Walkers have also been extensively kept out of water-catchment areas. This too is at its worst in the Peak District where the Water Authorities let the grouse moors for high rentals. And now the demands of the Service departments on the finest mountain and moorland in Britain are becoming voracious. Cader Idris and Dartmoor are in the news as I write, and no hill nor mountain seems safe. The Access to Mountains Act, 1939, which makes a case-by-case appeal necessary to gain access to wild country, is useless ; and fresh legislation is badly needed.

But if the interests which compete with the walker for the enjoyment of the hills were only exclusive, it would not be so bad. Most of them are destructive as well. I have said that man has done little to alter the shape of the hills ; and this is true seen against a geological background. But in the last hundred years he has systematically done all he can to foul his own nest. The hills have not escaped.

Water Authorities are again offenders : not only in creating large and ugly artificial lakes with sore edges and in drowning villages, but also in closing farms and in destroying the character of the hills with castellated cottages, cast-iron railings, park seats, ornamental conifers and other corporation amenities. Of the eleven major sheets of water of the Lake District,

Thirlmere and Haweswater have been devastated and Ennerdale is now doomed. Power schemes, particularly in the Highlands, have already destroyed or now threaten vast areas of mountain scenery. The aluminium works at Kinlochleven are only one of the many gigantic scars which disfigure the hills. An unenlightened policy of afforestation, now happily partially checked, has resulted in the mutilation of some of the finest Lakeland dales and in the strangling of the native Herdwick sheep farming. The tale of devastation is endless, where each interest is pursued, unco-ordinated and thoughtless of the others. Almost weekly *The Times* produces a splendid photograph of some well known scene of wild beauty doomed to death ; a few months later, when the disease has triumphed, the obituary notices appear. So topsy-turvy are our values in our strange civilisation that the argument that carries least weight is one in defence of beauty.

Great efforts, it is true, have been made by the National Trust and other bodies ; and large areas of hill and moor, most notably the whole core of the Lake District, have been acquired for the nation. But the recent outbreak of competitive grabbing of places of beauty emphasises the crying need for a strong and reasonable co-ordinated policy. No lover of the hills will deny the need for efficient lines of communication, a reasonable exploitation of our natural resources, the common amenities of life for the hill-dwellers, space for the war departments, water for cities and power for industry. All we ask is that these problems should be settled in relation to each other, and that the preservation of beauty, or rather its development —for beauty is no static thing—and access to it, should be the first and not the last consideration.

The establishment of National Parks, which is long overdue in this country, would do much to rationalise the whole question of the value of the precious hill districts. The outlook here is hopeful ; and if the report of Mr. John Dower on *The National Parks of England and Wales* and *National Parks : a Scottish Survey* are implemented it will be a great step in the right direction.

Whereas we can afford to treat the Lake District as a recreational area for the rest of England, the problem of the Highlands is a very different one, as it affects the whole economy of a mountain region. In the Lakes or Wales the preservation of the traditional form of farming is compatible with the foundation of National Parks. In the mountains of Scotland the ancient pastoral agriculture has long since broken down. The cattle which once helped to support a poor but vigorous tribal population have given place to sheep, deer and grouse. The lure of the colonies started the de-population of the land, but it was large-scale sheep farming that led to the early nineteenth-century evictions, the most notorious of which were the Sutherland Clearances, when the aged and infirm were ruthlessly ejected from their burning crofts. Later, when sporting rights became more profit-able, deer forest superseded sheep runs. In the second half of last century

THE VALE OF THE WHITE HORSE, BERKSHIRE
Water colour by Eric Ravilious, 1908-1942

nearly one-third of the total area of Scotland was strictly preserved as ground dedicated to the slaughter of deer. Paths and roads were closed, inns shut up and tenants were persecuted for showing their natural hospitality to travellers. In the famous Battle of Glen Tilt in 1845, Professor Balfour and a party of botanists who had been collecting specimens on Ben Macdhui were prosecuted by the Duke of Atholl for using an immemorial right of way. Even between the wars it was an added attraction to advertise an estate as "without tenants."

The tragic scene of deserted crofting townships, abandoned schools, ruined sheilings and profitless wastes of deer forest are a sad accompaniment of travel in the Highlands to-day. When the sporting trade was flourishing it brought much wealth to the north. But now not even profit for a few can be used as an argument against the complete economic reorganisation of the mountains of Scotland. Revived agriculture and fisheries, afforestation, improved communications and limited hydro-electric development might produce a prosperous mountain land with little sacrifice of beauty.

47

Before the war the importance of the part the hills were playing in the life of the community was already obvious. During the war the hills have contributed much to the training of our fighting forces. Not only have they been attractive places in which to let off live ammunition, as any war-time visitor to Snowdon is not likely to forget, but commando and assault troops were trained in mountaineering and rock-climbing. Mountain divisions, instructed by skilled mountaineers, were formed. The qualities of self-reliance, enterprise, discipline, endurance and friendly co-operation, essential to a good mountaineer, were felt to be just those qualities which were required in a modern warrior.

But the qualities which are bred by the impact of mountain beauty and mountain adventure can be of more value in peace than in war. Already various experiments in introducing boys of all sorts to the joys and rigours of the hills have been made. In this way not only can an unrivalled source of pleasure and content be revealed to them but in the revelation they will become better and happier members of our crowded society.

AUTHOR'S NOTE AND SHORT BIBLIOGRAPHY

The Ordinary Popular Editions of the 1" Ordnance Survey are excellent maps for the hills; but it is easier to visualise the modelling of the country from the special Tourist 1" coloured contour maps of the various hill districts. The Lakes and the Pentlands are also covered by special maps issued by Bartholomew. The only reasonable map for the complexities of the Black Cuillin is the Scottish Mountaineering Club's 3" sheet.

Detailed rock-climbing guide-books to the Lake District are published by the Fell and Rock Climbing Club and to North Wales by the Climbers' Club. More general mountaineering guides to the Highlands are published by the Scottish Mountaineering Club. The Pelican book *Climbing in Britain*, written by J. E. Q. Barford for the British Mountaineering Council, is a mine of information for walkers and climbers.

Many of the standard books of early hill travel have been referred to in the text. Amongst other works freely consulted are *Geology in the Service of Man*, 1944, by W. G. Fearnsides and O. M. B. Bulman; *Britain's Structure and Scenery*, 1946, by L. Dudley Stamp; *The Picturesque*, 1927, by Christopher Hussey; *Lake District History*, 1925, by W. G. Collingwood; *The Untutored Townsman's Invasion of the Country*, 1946, by C. E. M. Joad; *The Mountains of Snowdonia*, 1925, by H. R. C. Carr and G. A. Lister, and the Journals of the climbing and rambling clubs. *The Story of Scotland*, *The Story of Wales*, *British Weather*, *British Romantic Artists* and *English Water Colour Painters* in this series all deal more fully with matters which I have only touched upon.

Since this book was written, the establishment of National Parks has been brought a step nearer by the publication of the report of the National Parks Committee. It contains in an appendix a series of appreciations of the hill districts.

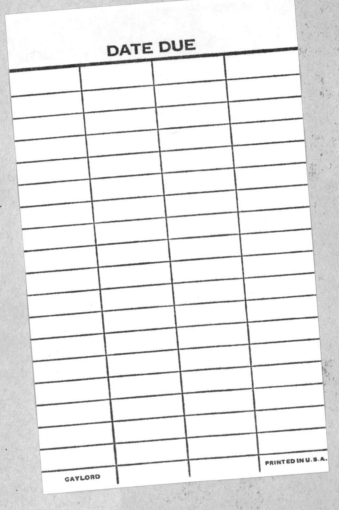

DATE DUE